Tunes for Clarinet Technic

LEVEL

by
Fred Weber
in collaboration with
Robert Lowry

To The Teacher

One of the most effective and enjoyable ways to develop technical dexterity on an instrument is through melodies of a technical nature, and with scale and rhythm variations based on familiar melodies. TUNES FOR TECHNIC is designed with this in mind. Because tunes, melodies and technical variations are interesting and more enjoyable to practice, most students will work more effectively, and over-all results will be greater. Some of the melodies and variations in TUNES FOR TECHNIC may be challenging and difficult. In this case work up slowly, and accurately, then gradually increase tempo. In general, the book progresses in difficulty and correlates with the method book, "The B♭ Clarinet Student," Part I. It may be also used in conjunction with any elementary B♭ Clarinet method.

The Belwin "STUDENT INSTRUMENTAL COURSE" - A course for individual and class instruction of LIKE instruments, at three levels, for all band instruments.

EACH BOOK IS COMPLETE IN ITSELF BUT ALL BOOKS ARE CORRELATED WITH EACH OTHER

METHOD
The "B♭ Clarinet Student" For individual or class instruction.

ALTHOUGH EACH BOOK CAN BE USED SEPARATELY, IDEALLY, ALL SUPPLEMENTARY BOOKS SHOULD BE USED AS COMPANION BOOKS WITH THE METHOD

STUDIES AND MELODIOUS ETUDES
Supplementary scales, warm-up and technical drills, musicianship studies and melody-like studies.

TUNES FOR TECHNIC
Technical type melodies, variations, and "famous passages" from musical literature --- for the development of technical dexterity.

THE B♭ CLARINET SOLOIST
Interesting and playable graded easy solo arrangements of famous and well-liked melodies. Also contains 2 Duets, and 1 Trio. Easy piano accompaniments.

DUETS FOR STUDENTS
Easy duet arrangements of familiar melodies for early ensemble experience.
Available for: Flute
B♭ Clarinet
Alto Sax
B♭ Cornet
Trombone

Contents

Title	Page
Adeste Fidelis	22
Alla Turca (Low Register) — *Mozart*	3
Alla Turca (High Register) — *Mozart*	8
America The Beautiful, Variation — *Ward*	23
Arkansas Traveler — *Folk Tune*	32
Auld Lang Syne	22
Band Played On, The — *Ward*	7
Banks Of The Little Eau Pleine	10
Bat Waltz, The — *Strauss*	30
Bicycle Built For Two — *Dacre*	9
Blow The Man Down	24
Blue Bells Of Scotland, The	15
Camptown Races — *Foster*	9
Can Can — *Offenbach*	21
Cara Nome — *Verdi*	19
Carnival Of Venice And Variations	28
Comin' Round The Mountain	15
Crusaders' Hymn	5
Dance — *Folk Song*	8
Dance Etude — *Streabbog*	29
Down In The Valley	4
Drink To Me Only In B♭	27
Drink To Me Only In C — *English Air*	4
Drink To Me Only In C	8
Durang's Hornpipe	32
Dying Cowboy, The	19
Emperor Waltz — *J. Strauss*	24
English Melody	14
Erie Canal, The — *Work Song*	14
Father Of Victory March — *Ganne*	21
Fiesta	13
Garden Dance, The — *Flemish Folk Song*	5
German Waltz — *Folk Song*	8
Greensleeves	29
Happy Dance — *Purcell*	29
Here We Go Looby Lou	3
Home Sweet Home	11
Hungarian Dance Theme — *Brahms*	10
Hymn Of Thanksgiving	22
I Love You Truly — *Bond*	6
I'm A Poor Wayfaring Stranger	10
Irene	5
Jewish Folk Song	23
Joyce's 71st Regiment — *Boyer*	11

Title	Page
Loch Lomond	15
Long, Long Ago	13
March By Mozart — *Mozart*	31
Marines' March And Variation	20
Massa's In De Cold, Cold Ground — *S. Foster*	25
Melody — *Rubinstein*	17
Melody By Borodin — *Borodin*	25
Melody In Key Of D	24
Melody From The Opera Carmen — *Bizet*	32
Minuet — *Mozart*	26
Moment Musical — *Schubert*	30
Noah's Ark — *College Song*	27
Onward Christian Soldiers	7
Peasant Dance — *Folk Song*	3
Poet And Peasant Melody — *Von Suppe*	6
Polly Wolly Doodle And Variation	20
Pop Goes The Weazel	4
Rainbow Theme — *Chopin*	11
Roses From The South — *J. Strauss*	17
Russian Melody	14
Sailor's Hornpipe	30
Sakura, Sakura — *Japanese Folk Song*	19
Sharpshooters' March — *Metalo*	19
She'll Be Comin' Round The Mountain — *Traditional*	12
S.I.B.A. March — *Hall*	17
Sleeping Beauty Waltz — *Tschaikowsky*	12
Sonatina — *Beethoven*	26
Swanee River	9
Tell Me Why	7
Theme From High School Cadets March — *Sousa*	11
Theme From High School Cadets March — *Sousa*	12
Theme From The Thunderer March — *Sousa*	29
Theme And Variations — *Nursery Rhyme*	18
Tschaikowsky Concerto Theme — *Tschaikowsky*	25
Under The Double Eagle	21
Up On The Housetop	15
Variations On A Famous Theme — *Mozart*	16
Variations On Yankee Doodle	31
Violins Play, The — *Paganini*	23
Waltz Melody — *Nageli*	6
Waltz Viennese — *Strauss*	26
We Wish You A Merry Christmas	14
Yankee Doodle In C	6
Yankee Doodle In F	3
Young May Moon, The	27

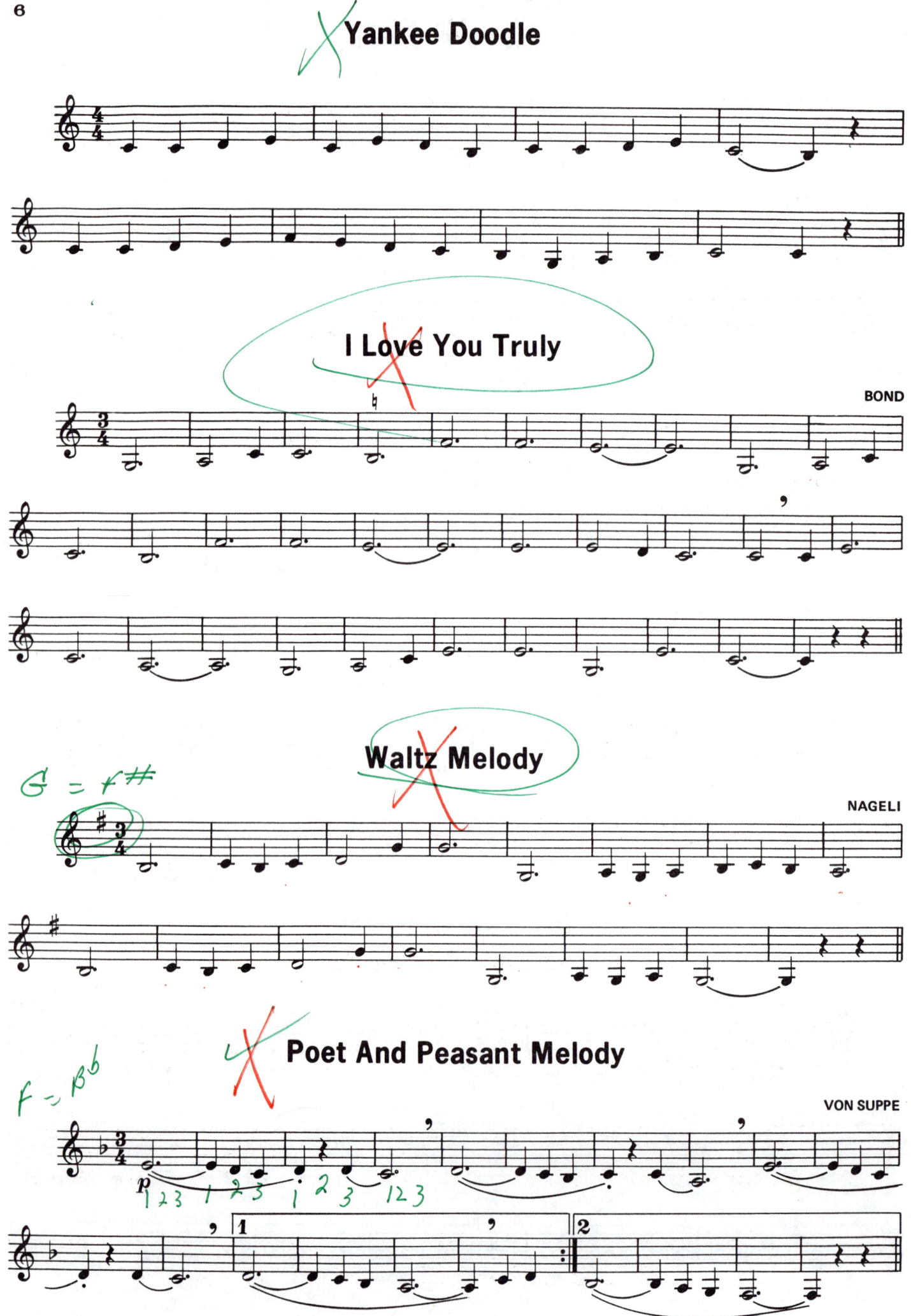

Tell Me Why

Onward Christian Soldiers March

Play in an accented style

The Band Played On

WARD

8

German Waltz
FOLK SONG

Drink To Me Only

Alla Turca
(High Register)

MOZART

Dance
FOLK SONG

B.I.C.108

Bicycle Built For Two

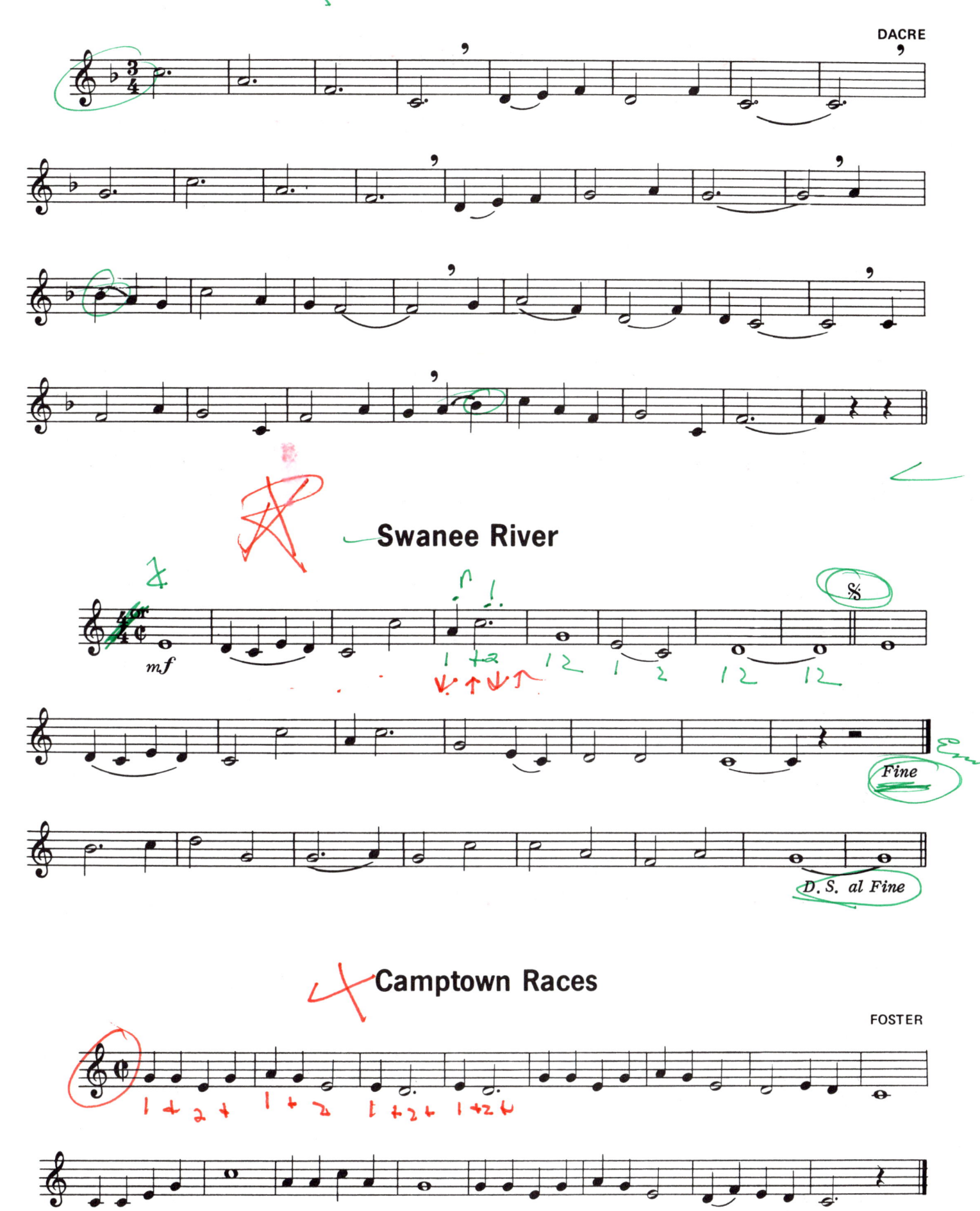

DACRE

Swanee River

Camptown Races

FOSTER

Hungarian Dance Theme

I'm A Poor Wayfaring Stranger

The Banks Of The Little Eau Pleine

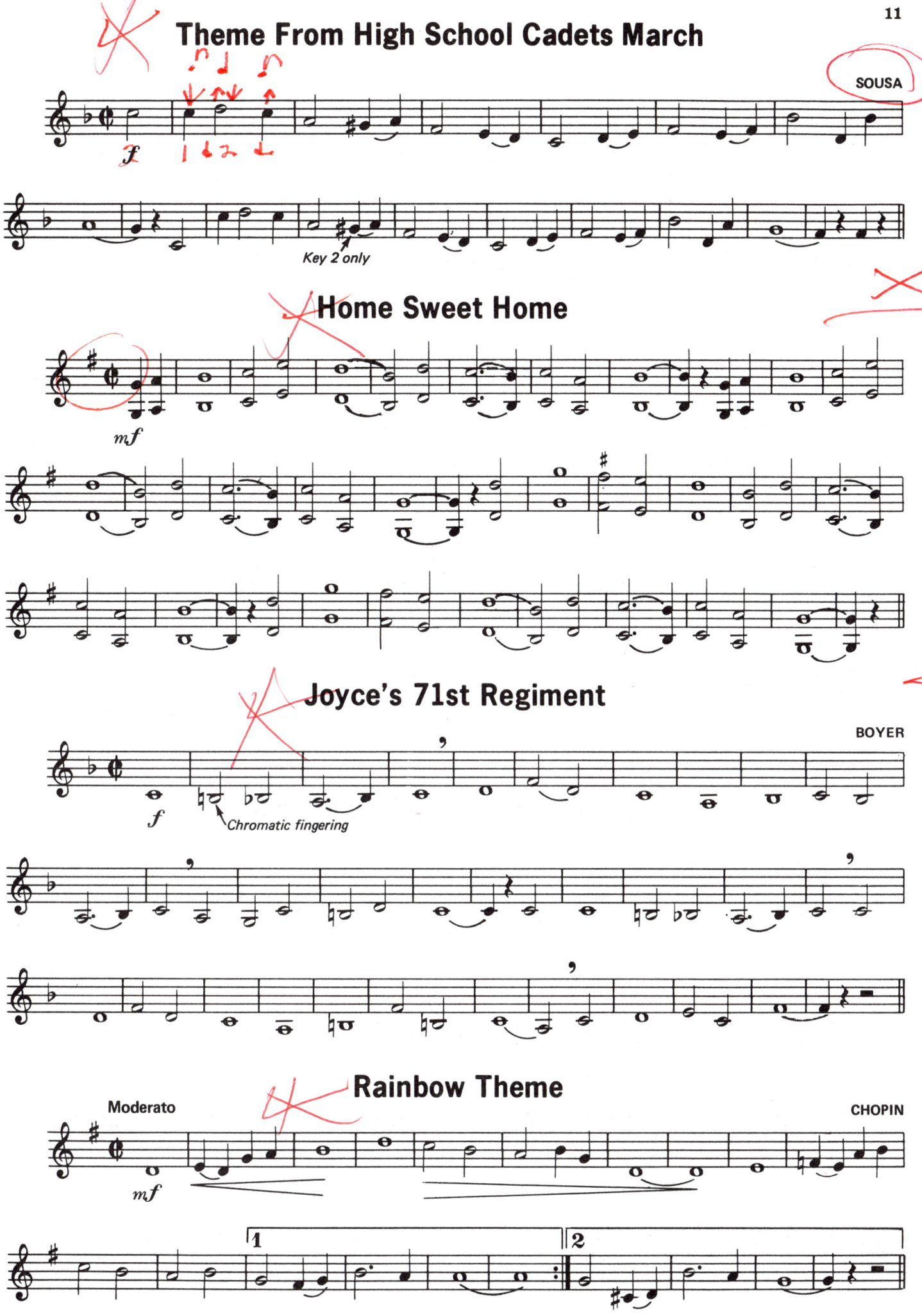

Theme From High School Cadets March

SOUSA

Home Sweet Home

Joyce's 71st Regiment

BOYER

Chromatic fingering

Rainbow Theme

Moderato

CHOPIN

B.I.C.108

Sleeping Beauty Waltz

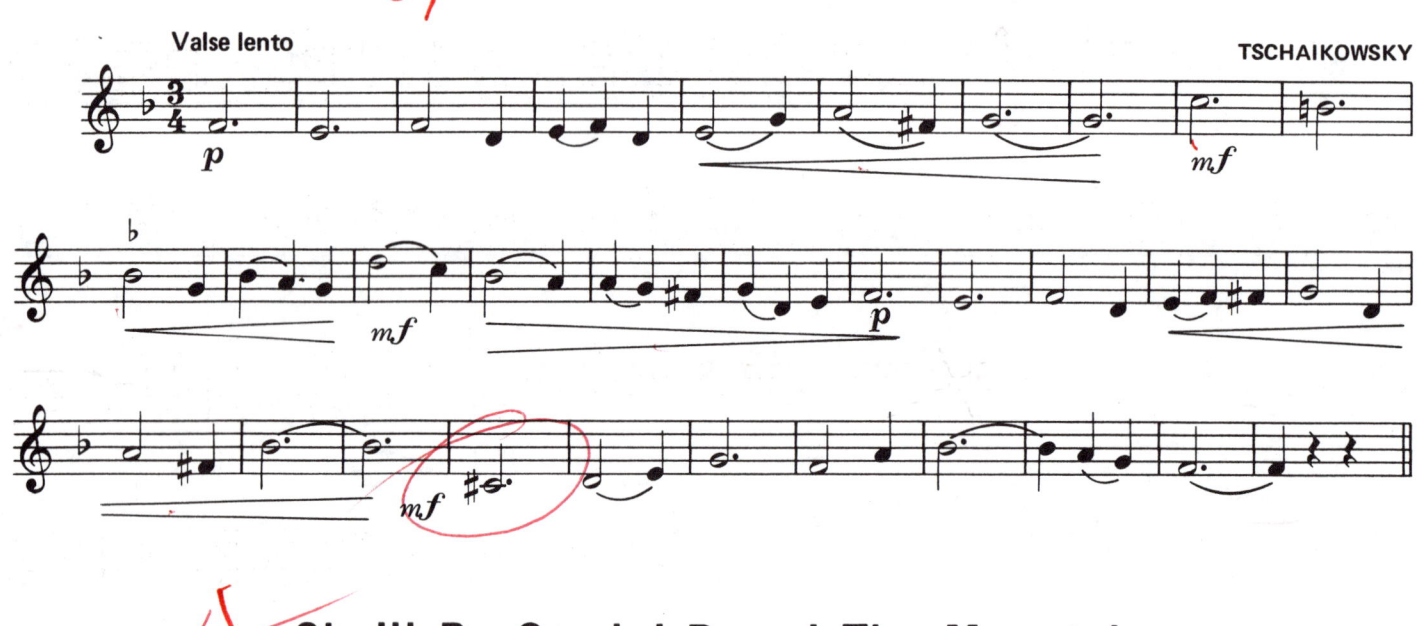

She'll Be Comin' Round The Mountain

Theme From High School Cadets March

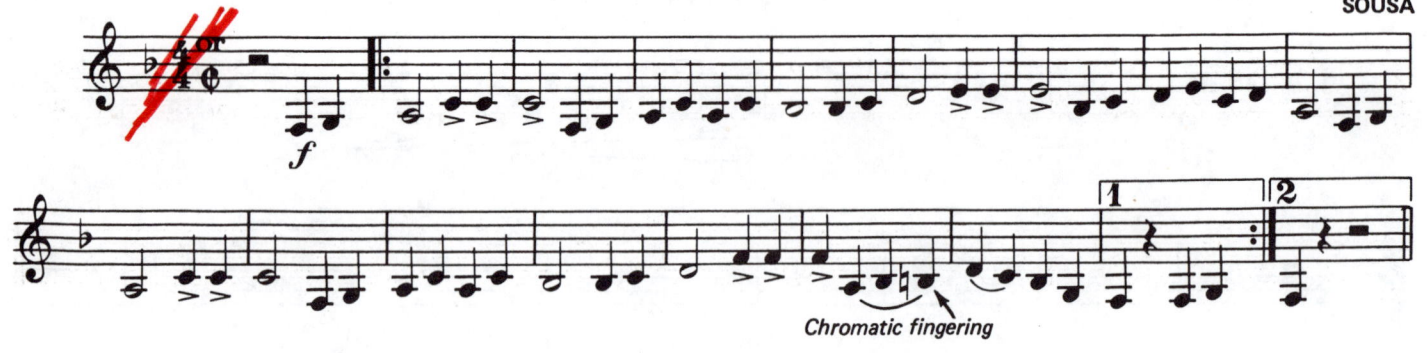

Fiesta

Long Long Ago

Russian Melody

We Wish You A Merry Christmas

English Melody

The Erie Canal

WORK SONG

Up On The Housetop

Comin' Round The Mountain

Loch Lomond

The Blue-Bells Of Scotland

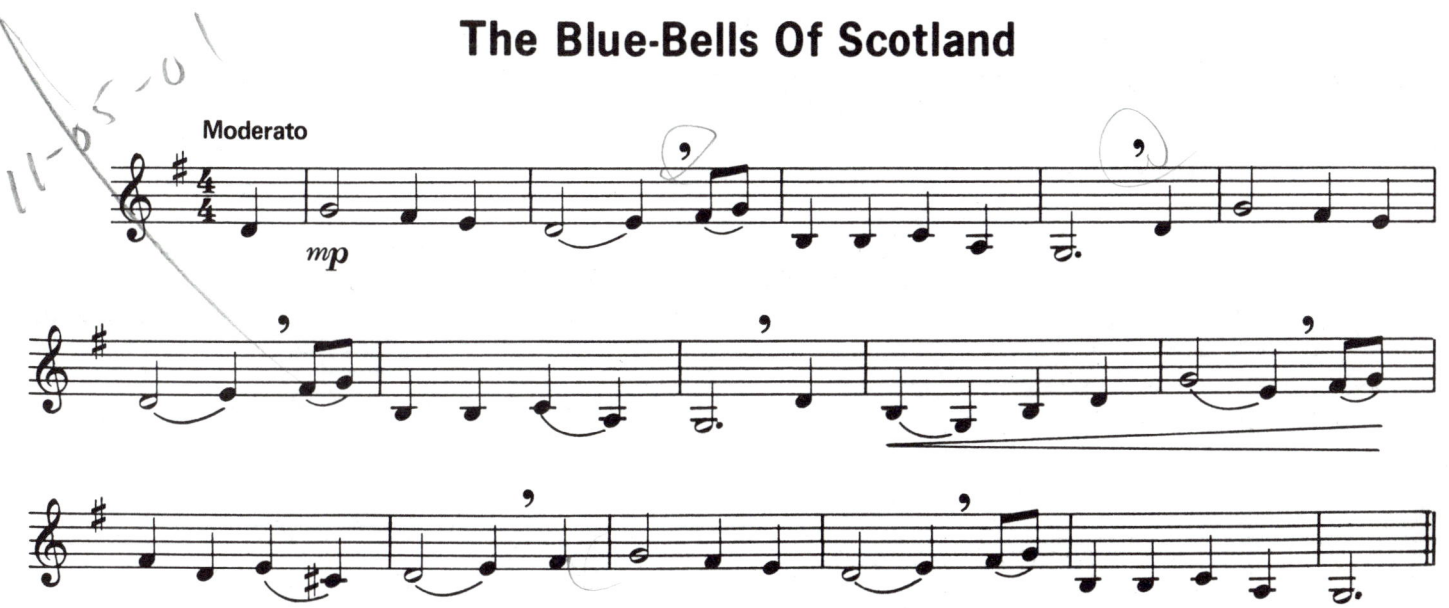

Carnival Of Venice With Variations

Rhythm Variation

Slowly - 6 beats per measure

Slowly

March tempo

Scale Variation
Work out carefully, then try for speed.

B.I.C.108

Variation On Yankee Doodle

Work out carefully, then try for speed.

March By Mozart

Work out carefully, then try for speed.

MOZART

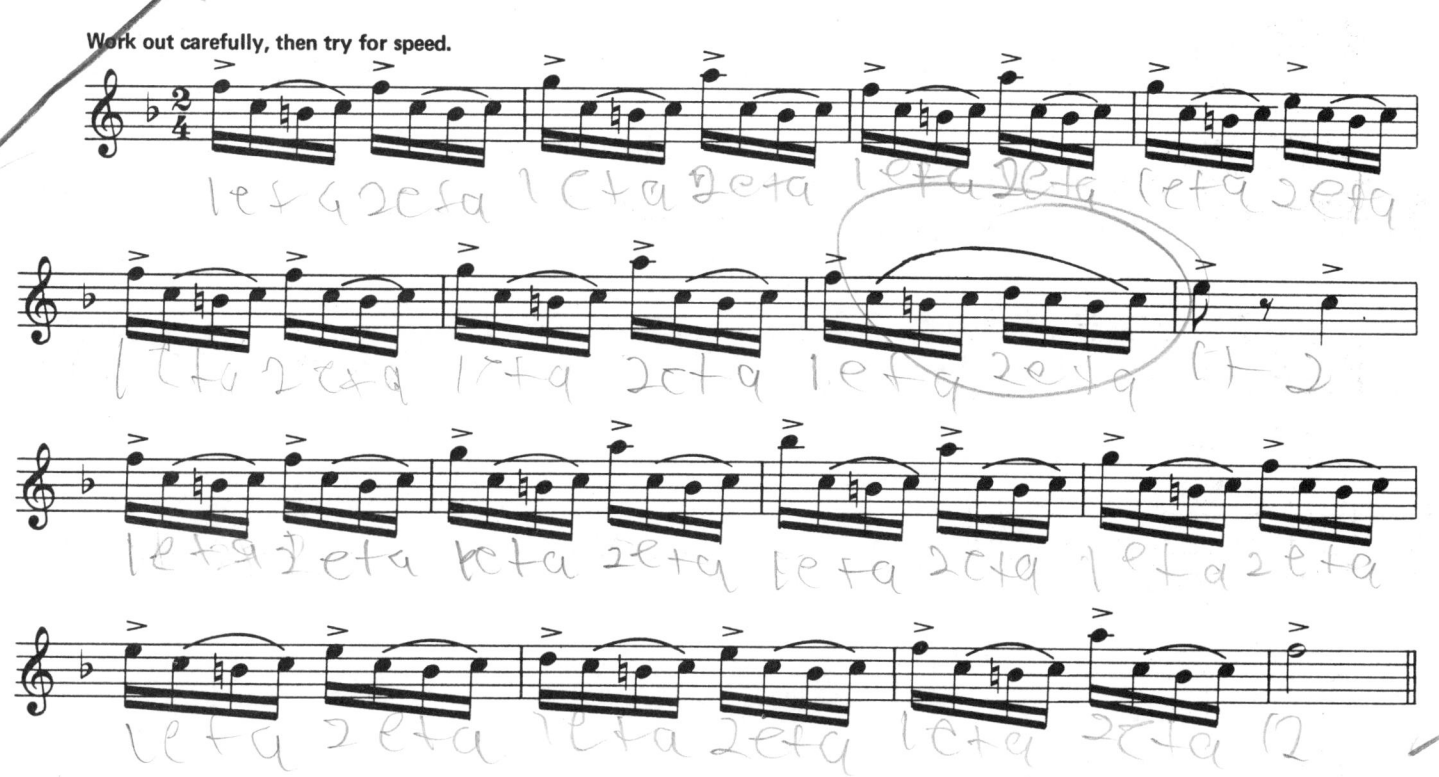

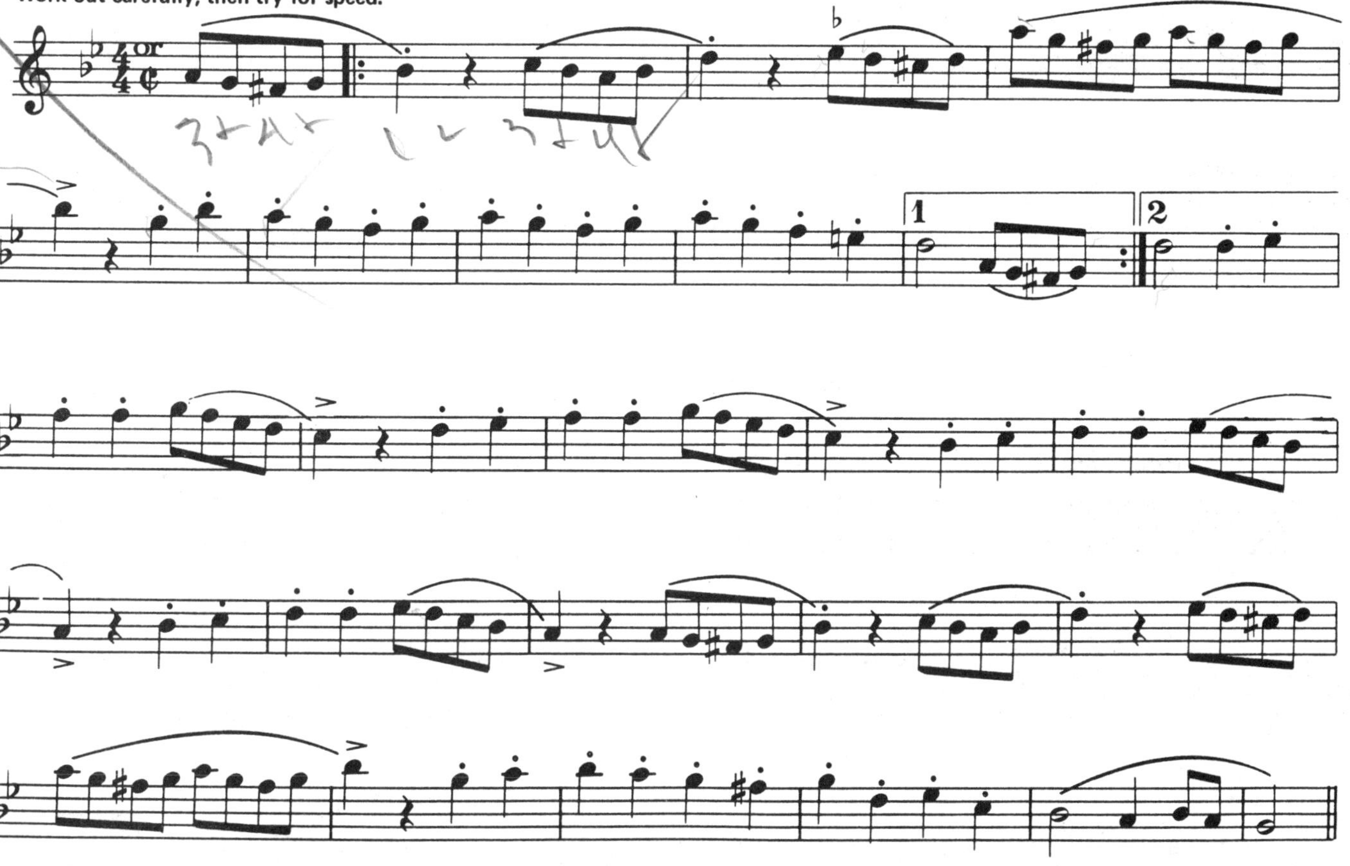